SERIES EDITOR: SYDNEY WOOD

Understanding
People in the Past

Settlers of Scotland

D1638334

ELIZABETH CURTIS
& KIM DAVIDSON

Hodder & Stoughton
A MEMBER OF THE HODDER HEADLINE GROUP

This book is about Scotland a very long time ago. You will find out about the people who lived here from the first settlers until Scotland became one kingdom. You will also find out about some of the discoveries which made people's lives better.

The people in this book lived so long ago that it is easier to think of them being around *so many thousand* years ago. People call a thousand years a millenium. A hundred years is a century and ten years is a decade.

Sometimes people use BC and AD when they talk about dates. This is a way of counting dates from the year Jesus Christ was born. BC means *Before Christ*. AD comes from the Latin words *anno domini*, meaning *in the year of the lord*. People who study history often talk about dates BP which means *before the present*.

Contents

Finding Out About the Past

Most of the people in this book lived before history books were written. So we have to look for other kinds of clues to tell us about people in the past. These clues are called **evidence**. Have a look at the pictures here. What kind of clues can you find about the past?

There are two kinds of people who help us to find out about life long ago.

Historians study things people wrote about when and where they lived.

Archaeologists look at all the things people have made in the past. They use lots of different kinds of evidence to help them.

▲ Source 1
Sometimes the remains of ancient buildings can still be seen today, like these at Skara Brae in Orkney.

▼ Source 2
Some people find things in the ground. This young archaeologist found a 4000 year-old flint arrowhead at Newburgh, Aberdeenshire.

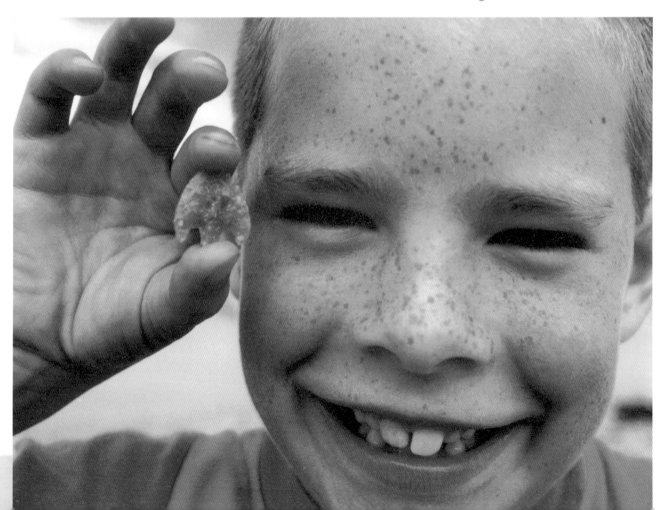

Source 3 ▶
The outline of very old walls can be seen from the air, like this hillfort at Traprain Law in the South of Scotland.

▼ **Source 4**
Sometimes archaeologists collect soil in a long tube. They look at the soil under a microscope. They can work out what kind of plants grew in the past.

Close your eyes! Imagine a land completely covered in snow and ice where very little can live. This is what Scotland was like over 10 000 years ago. Very, very slowly, as the air became warmer, the ice began to melt. A land of flat topped mountains, deep valleys, rivers and lochs appeared above the sea.

Two thousand years passed. The weather became more like we know it now. Animals ate the new shoots and lived deep in the forests which covered most of Scotland. Still there were no people.

▲ **Source 1**
Scotland once looked like this.

▼ **Source 2**
Birch trees like the ones here grew long ago. Elk, deer and wild cattle roamed the forests, as well as wolves and bears.

pine tree

elk

birch tree

deer

Nobody is sure why the first people came north. Perhaps some followed the herds of animals in search of food. Others may have come up the coast in small round boats called **coracles**. The first visitors to Scotland found plenty of animals to hunt and lots of plants, sea food, nuts and berries to eat. But these people were not farmers. They wandered about, looking for food. You can find out more about their way of life in Chapter 3.

▼ **Source 3**
Much of Scotland was covered with forest.

▲ **Source 4**
Some people may have arrived in coracles.

Imagine that you are one of the first people to come to Scotland. What would you need to help you to survive?

A C T I V I T I E S

Hunter Gatherers

▲ Source 1
Archaeologists dig to find evidence of people living on the island of Rum 9000 years ago.

▼ Source 2
This is an anorak made of sealskin. People in Scotland about 9000 years ago probably wore clothes like this.

About 9000 years ago some of the first settlers in Scotland came to the island of Rum off the west coast. They hunted animals for food. They also used the animal bones and skins to make tools and clothes. They gathered nuts and berries to eat as well. Archaeologists call the time when these hunter gatherer people lived the **Mesolithic**.

Archaeologists looking for evidence found sharp tools used by early settlers on Rum. But it is difficult to find evidence for people living so long ago. This is because people did not stay in one place for a long time. Many of their belongings were made out of materials which rot away, like wood and animal skins.

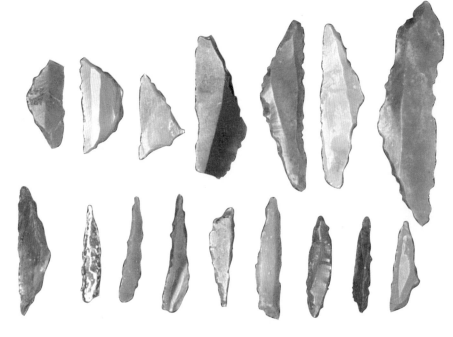

▲ Source 3
The early people made these tools. They are made from two very sharp stones called flint and bloodstone. Bloodstone is a green stone with red marks, like drops of blood.

▼ Source 4

These drawings show what archaeologists think life might have been like for a group of people about 9000 years ago. Look carefully at the clothes they are wearing, the tools they are working with and the food they are eating. Everything is made from natural materials.

1 The hunters spot a stag in a clearing. They silently take aim and kill it.

2 They tie the stag's legs together and fasten it to a long pole. They take it back to the family camp.

3 There is great excitement back at camp. Everybody sets to work with sharp flint knives and scrapers to butcher the stag.

4 All of the animal is useful. There is fresh meat to eat, skin for clothes and shelter, bones and antler for tools and jewellery.

5 In the evening there is a feast of roast venison with freshly gathered fruits, nuts and wild mushrooms. The older people tell stories about their journeys.

6 It is time to go. The deer are on the move and the salmon have swum away. The hunters load their belongings on to long wooden frames, ready for their next journey.

Work in a group and make a short play about the day you caught a great stag.

A C T I V I T I E S

The First Farmers

People who had learned to plant seeds every year came to Scotland. They could stay in one place and make proper homes. They were the first farmers.

1 The wooden plough digs up the land so the farmers can sow the seeds.

2 The farmers keep oxen to do the heavy work.

3 The farmers grind the ripe corn grains on a **quernstone**. Now they have flour.

4 The flour is mixed with water. It is cooked over the fire to make bread.

◀ Source 1
Early farming.

The change from hunting and gathering food to farming is one of the most important in history. Why? What caused this change? Think about these things:

Moving around to find food was tiring.

Sometimes there was not enough food.

It was difficult to store and carry food.

Hunting was often dangerous.

▲ Source 2
Everyone in the village is busy.

No one knows for certain how farming began. Perhaps settlers from other lands brought new ideas such as keeping animals and growing grain. Or things may have happened almost by accident. People discovered that keeping animals made life much easier. They could kill their own animals for food. Animal hides and wool made warm clothes for the winter. When trees and stones were cleared away, seed could be sown to grow crops. The grain could be ground into flour to make bread.

People could settle in one place and they lived in warm houses built of stone and wood.

People who lived between 6000 and 4000 years ago are known as **Neolithic**.

Imagine that you are one of the early farmers in Scotland. Write and draw pictures about how life has changed for you and your family.

A C T I V I T I E S

Living in a Neolithic House

Our family live in Skara Brae, by the sand dunes by the sea. There are eight stone houses in our village. We are all farmers. Most things in our house are made of stone because there are hardly any trees on this island. We have a fireplace in the middle of our house and stone bed boxes to sleep in. Even our kitchen cupboard is made of stone.

Today my brother and I are working in the house. I find grinding grain on this quernstone very tiring. Sometimes we go out fishing. We store fish in a stone box by the fire. The village potter makes pots for cooking in and for storing food and water. In the middle of our village is a meeting place. The men go there to talk about our crops and animals.

▲ **Source 1**
A Neolithic house at Skara Brae, Orkney.

After about 600 years of people living there, sand dunes began to cover over the village. Eventually, all of the houses were covered in sand and nobody could live there any more. About 100 years ago, a big storm made the sand blow away, uncovering the remains of the 5000 year old village.

▼ Source 2
This is what a Skara Brae house looks like today.

LOOKING AT THE EVIDENCE

1 **In groups compare Source 1 to Sources 2 and 3.**

   Discuss what is the same and what is different.

2 **Record what you find out under these headings:**

   THINGS WHICH SURVIVE
   THINGS WHICH DO NOT SURVIVE

   What kind of materials survive and what kind of materials do not? Can you think why?

3 **In your groups draw a picture of the inside of a house at Skara Brae. Put yourselves in it doing different tasks. Label the drawing to show objects you are wearing and using and the furniture in your house.**

ACTIVITIES

▲ Source 3
These are just some of the things which were found in the houses at Skara Brae – carved stone balls, pins, necklaces and pendants made of whalebone and walrus tusk.

Balbridie Timber Hall

The houses at Skara Brae are made of stone. Most people in the rest of Scotland lived in wooden houses. These cannot be seen today. Can you think why?

Archaeologists found the remains of a wooden house in Aberdeenshire which was built about the same time as Skara Brae. All that is left of Balbridie Hall today are the holes and slots in the ground that the timber poles went into. By looking at the pictures and text here you can find out more about what the house once looked like.

▲ Source 1
The remains of Balbridie Timber Hall, seen from the air.

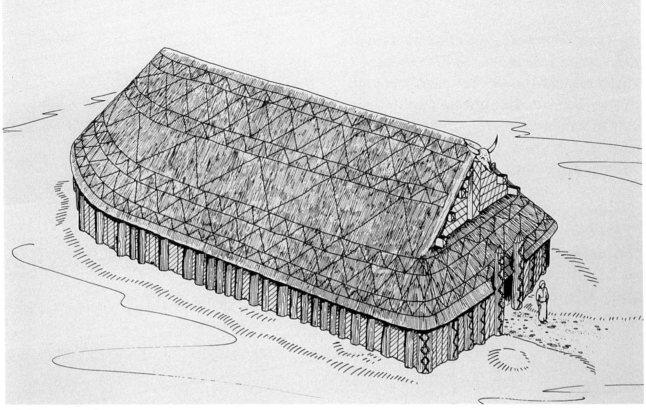

▲ Source 2

This is what one artist thinks the Hall might have looked like.

1 **Look carefully at the photograph of the remains of Balbridie. The people who built it used different kinds of wooden posts.**

There were cylinder shaped posts like this:

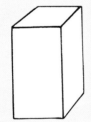 **There were cuboid shaped posts like this.**

2 **Compare Sources 1 and 2.**

Which parts are drawn from evidence and which parts has the artist made up?

3 **Think back to Skara Brae.**

Is Balbridie bigger or smaller than one house at Skara?

How many people do think could have lived inside Balbridie? Give a reason for your answer.

4 **Using the photograph of Balbridie and what you have learned from Skara Brae draw what you think the hall might have looked like inside.**

A C T I V I T I E S

Cairns of the Dead

About 5000 years ago the early farmers started to build big stone mounds. These are called **cairns.** Cairns were not always the same size but they were built for the same reason. Important people were placed inside them when they died. They were laid in a room called a chamber. Stones were piled round the chamber to make the mound. In some cairns the bones of dogs and deer have been found. Experts think that this shows the people who once lived there held feasts. Why do you think they went to so much trouble to bury their dead?

▲ **Source 1**
This is Maes Howe Chambered Cairn in Orkney. It is a huge pudding basin shape.

▼ **Source 2**
This is Camster Long Cairn in Caithness. It is like a giant body lying on the ground.

▲ **Source 3**
This cairn at Isbister, Orkney, is known as the Tomb of the Eagles. When it was opened up, bones of sea eagles were found alongside the bones of 324 people.

▲ **Source 4**
This is a modern cemetery. How is this the same as the cairns? How is it different?

1 **The people who built cairns wanted to remember their families and their leaders.**
How do we remember people of the past today? Make a list of all the ways that you can think of.

2 **The burial cairns like Camster reminded people of their ancestors. Ancestors are people in your family born before you were. Try to find out more about your own ancestors and then make your own family tree like the one here.**

In this tree you are the living part of it at the top. The more ancestors you can find, the longer the roots of your tree will be.

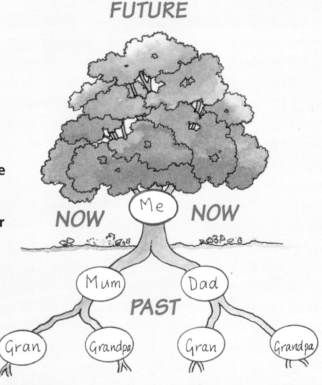

ACTIVITIES

17

Stone Circles

The early farmers also built circles of huge stones. The pictures here show some of the different kinds of stone circles from around Scotland.

▲ Source 1
This is Callanish Stone Circle, on the Island of Lewis, off the West Coast of Scotland. Pathways of standing stones lead the way to the small circle of stones in the middle.

▼ Source 2
This is the Ring of Brodgar in Orkney. It is surrounded by a ditch in the earth, called a henge.

Big stones like these are called **megaliths**.

Mega = huge
Lith = stone

▲ **Source 3**
In this stone circle the biggest stone lies on its side. It is in Aberdeenshire and is called the East Aquhorthies Recumbent Stone Circle.

These circles are all about 5000 years old. They are all different. This is because each village of people carefully chose each stone and made their own designs. Archaeologists think that people used the circles to worship their gods. They prayed and gave thanks for good harvests. In many parts of Scotland people used them at sunrise and sunset. In the North East of Scotland, many stone circles have one stone which lies on its side. This is called a **recumbent** stone. The circles were used in the same way as those at Callanish and Brodgar. There is one big difference. The recumbent stone is always in the South West of the Circle. Archaeologists think that this was so that the farmers could watch the moon rise above it. So celebrations in the North East like at East Aquhorthies would take place after sunset.

▲ **Source 4**
You can see the circle of stones clearly in this picture of Brodgar from the air.

We need your help to build our village recumbent stone circle.

Investigate these things:

How can you mark out the circle?

How can you move heavy stones?

How can you place a huge heavy stone upright?

A C T I V I T I E S

The First Metal Workers

9

Over 5000 years ago, people used fire to heat and mould jewellery from pieces of gold, silver and copper they found in the ground.

Then, about 4000 years ago, some people discovered that if you melt tin and copper together you get a much stronger metal called **bronze**. Bronze axes had a sharper cutting edge than the old stone ones. But even bronze was not as good as flintstone for making some things like arrowheads.

▲ **Source 1**

This stone axe mould is about 4000 years old. It was found by a farmer ploughing his field. The mould is broken, which is probably why it was thrown away. The axe head in the mould is bronze. It is called a flat axe.

▼ **Source 2**

MAKING BRONZE

1

This man is paddling his coracle up the River Don. He is a metal worker who travels from village to village. He carries with him all he needs for making bronze tools and ornaments.

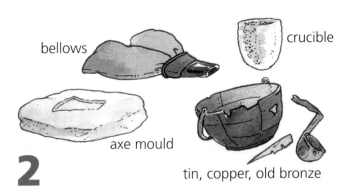

2

He has pieces of tin and copper to make into bronze, and some clay pots called **crucibles** for melting the metals in. He also carries a mould for making axes.

Some people think I can work magic because I can melt down metal and change it into a different shape.

It is very hot work! I use a leather bellows to get the fire started, and to keep it hot until the metal is runny enough to pour into my mould.

As well as tools and weapons, I can make beautiful jewellery. Sometimes I use gold as well as bronze.

3

The mould is made of stone so that it will not be destroyed by the heat of the molten bronze.

4

When the metal has cooled it is very hard. The metalworker levers it carefully out of the mould.

Source 3 ▶

The grave is lined and covered with stone. Archaeologists call these graves **cists**.

My husband died of a fever. At last his tomb is ready. We will leave him with all he needs for his next life. My husband was a good farmer and a brave hunter. I have placed a drink by him in a clay beaker. I have put his bow and arrow and dagger in, too.

▼ Source 4

4000 years ago people would have known and used all these things. Some of them were found in graves beside a dead person, like the man in Source 3.

carved stone ball

gold jewellery

flint arrowheads

clay beaker

1 Can you think why the flat axe in Source 1 got its name?

2 Look carefully at the objects in Source 4. Are they all made of metal? Give a reason for your answer.

3 Make a flat axe mould with clay or plasticine. Fill the mould with plaster like the metalworker did to make the axe.

4 Wooden handles of things like axes do not survive, because wood rots in the ground. Investigate ways of joining your moulded axe head to a handle.

A C T I V I T I E S

Forts and Farms

The map on page 23 shows where some people were living in Scotland about 2000 years ago. It also shows the different kinds of homes that they lived in.

Some of the most powerful people built themselves forts to live in. Others had huge stone towers called **brochs** built as part of their village like Gurness in Orkney. Some built their homes on stilts in lochs, like Kenmore in Perthshire. These are called **crannogs**.

To show how important and brave they were some people sent out warriors to raid nearby farms. The farmers lived in villages in round wooden houses next to their fields, like Kinnord in Aberdeenshire.

Find each kind of home on the map of Scotland.

▲ **Source 1**
Powerful people built forts with villages enclosed by steep walls up on hills, like these on two hills in Angus. They are known as the White Caterthun and the Brown Caterthun. The rings around the hilltops show where the huge walls once stood. The inside wall of the White Caterthun was twelve metres thick!

▼ **Source 2**
Archaeologists are re-building a crannog on Loch Tay. This photograph was taken before the thatched roof was put on. The archaeologists think that about twelve people lived there. The crannog was easily defended because it was on the water. People could get to it by using a wooden walkway or by boat. The people who lived here farmed the land near the shore and fished in the loch.

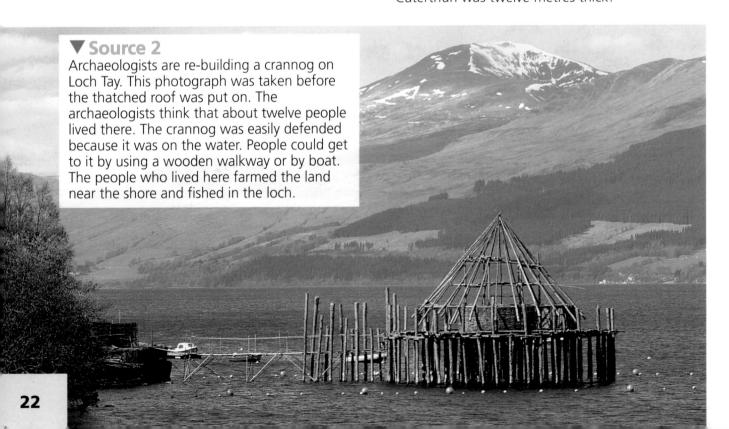

▼ Source 3

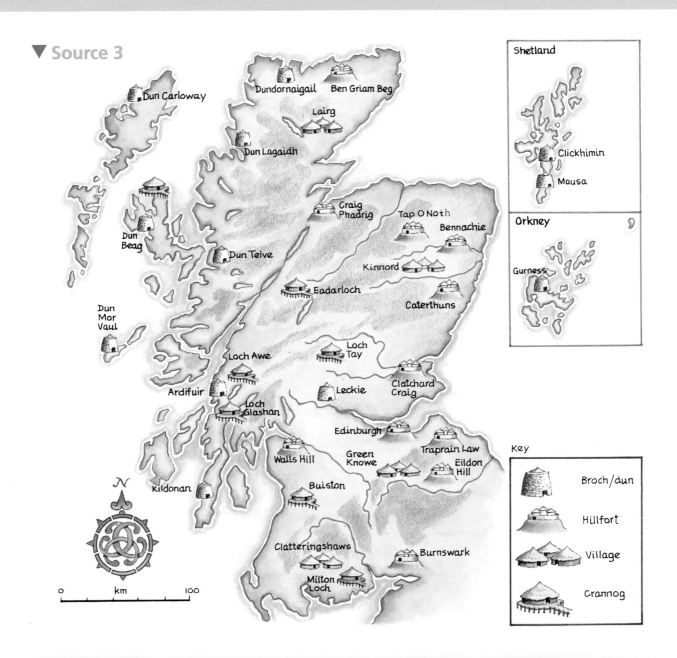

Copy the table below and put a tick in a box when you agree with its feature and a cross when you disagree.

	on water	defended	near farmland	1 family lived here	more than 1 family lived here	easily seen
crannog						
hillfort						
village						
broch						

A C T I V I T I E S

The Romans Invade Scotland

By the year 78 AD, South Britain had been ruled by the Romans for over 30 years. The Romans had built large farms, towns and a network of roads. The Romans had a huge empire in Europe, Africa and Egypt. Their soldiers were well trained.

In 78 AD, the Roman Emperor Vespasian decided that he wanted to conquer the rest of the British Isles. So he sent his Governor Agricola to Scotland to fight the Caledonians for their land.

The people living in Scotland at that time knew about the Romans. Some of the richer native people traded with them. The tribes in Scotland were used to fighting each other to get more land. So each tribe had its own trained warriors.

Ave! My name is Agricola. I am Governor of Britain. It is my job to conquer all the people of this country so that it will stay part of the Roman Empire. I have come north to fight the brave tribe of the Caledonians. We will soon meet at the hill of Mons Graupius, in the North East part of Scotland.

▲ Source 2

I am Calgacus, leader of the Caledonians, the tribe from the north. My name means The Swordsman. We shall fight the Romans for our freedom and show them what great warriors we are.

▲ Source 3

Ave! I am Cornelius Tacitus. I am married to Agricola's daughter. Agricola told me of the great battle of Mons Graupius when he returned to Rome. I wrote down his story so that people like you could learn all about it.

▲ Source 4

▲ Source 1
A Roman soldier.

▼ Source 5

This is what Tacitus wrote:

THE CALEDONIANS HAD THE BIGGER ARMY. ON THE SLOPES OF THE HILL THEIR FOOT WARRIORS ARMED WITH LONG SWORDS AND SMALL SHIELDS FACED AGRICOLA'S MEN. ON THE FLATTER GROUND CALEDONIAN CHARIOTEERS BATTLED WITH THE ROMAN CAVALRY. THE CAVALRY CHARGED WITH ALL THEIR MIGHT AND SCATTERED THE CHARIOTEERS. CALGACUS' MEN TRIED TO SURPRISE THE ROMAN FOOT SOLDIERS FROM BEHIND. BUT IT WAS NO GOOD. THE CALEDONIANS COULD NOT MATCH THE SKILL OF THE ROMANS. WHEN AGRICOLA'S MEN WERE TIRED OF KILLING, THE BATTLE ENDED. THE CALEDONIANS LOST 10 000 MEN, AGRICOLA ONLY 360.

1 Imagine you are one of the Caledonians who escaped. Make up the story you would go back and tell your family after the battle.

2 Tacitus wrote nearly 2000 years ago. He wrote down what Agricola told him after the battle. Why do you think he made the Caledonians seem so brave?

A C T I V I T I E S

▼ Source 6

At the start of the battle, there were many more Caledonians than Romans. The Caledonians faced downhill. The Romans faced uphill. The Caledonians fought hard. But the Romans won. Can you think why?

MONS GRAUPIUS

Caledonians

Caledonians

Caledonian chariots

Caledonian chariots

Trumpet (called a Carnyx)

Roman foot soldiers

Caledonians

Roman cavalry

Roman standard bearer

Roman cavalry

Building the Antonine Wall

Ave! I am the Emperor Antoninus. It is nearly 100 years since Agricola fought the Caledonians. I want to be a famous conqueror. I sent my Governor Lollius Urbicus to defeat the tribes in the south of Scotland. In the year 140 AD I commanded him to build a wall to defend my Empire from the tribes of the north. Some local people come to trade their goods for imported Roman products. Some of my soldiers have married women from nearby tribes. It is now a time of peace.

The Antonine Wall was completed in 143 AD. It went from the Forth across to the Clyde. It took three Legions of soldiers two years to build it. Each Legion put in special stones called Distance Slabs in the wall to show how much of the wall they finished.

◀ **Source 1**

▼ **Source 2**

This is a drawing of how the wall was made. It was built of turf on a stone base. In front of the wall was a deep ditch. There was probably a wooden fence running along the top. Why do you think the Romans dug the deep ditch?

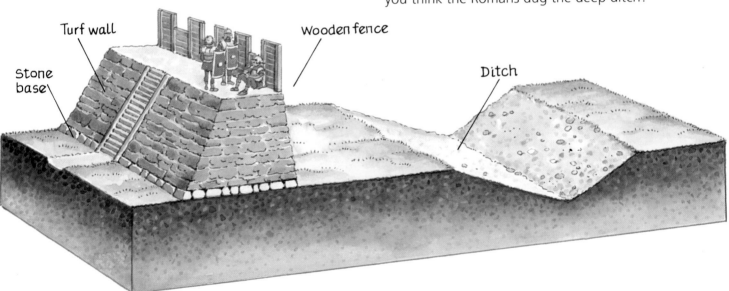

Turf wall   Wooden fence

Stone base   Ditch

We need your help to build the next section of the wall.

Look carefully at Source 2. Work in groups to plan how you would make a model of part of the wall. Test your plan to see how well it works.

ACTIVITIES

▲ **Source 3**

This stone was put in the Wall by the Roman soldiers of the Second Legion. They built one stretch of the Wall. The Romans measured in paces, which were about the same as our metres. The Second Legion's stretch of Wall measured 4652 paces. Can you find the number on the stone?

The picture on the stone is as important as the writing. Most people could not read or write so the pictures tell the same story. The stone was found near Bridgeness. It is now kept in the National Museum of Scotland in Edinburgh.

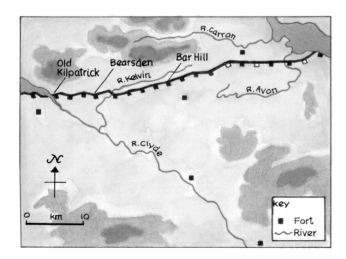

▲ **Source 4**

Look where the Romans built their wall. Why do you think they chose this place?

LOOKING AT EVIDENCE

1 **Discuss what you think is happening at the left hand side of the distance slab. Who do you think the picture is meant for, and why?**

2 **The right-hand side of the slab shows the Romans making an offering to their gods. They are going to kill some animals. What kind of animals are they?**

3 **The kneeling man has a knife. What is he about to do?**

4 **The Romans used letters instead of numbers. Can you work out the numbers on the stone? This is what the letters mean:**

$$\text{ⅠⅠⅠⅠ} = 4000 \qquad C = 100$$
$$L = 50$$
$$D = 500 \qquad I = 1$$

(Clue: sometimes you have to add numbers together. For example: II = 2)

Where else do you sometimes see Roman numbers today?

A C T I V I T I E S

27

Living on the Antonine Wall

By looking at the remains of many forts along the Antonine Wall, experts can work out what life was like. In the plan in Source 4 you can see where the soldiers lived at Bearsden Fort. Eight soldiers shared a room in a building called a barrack.

Soldiers were not allowed to marry according to Roman law. But they could marry by local custom. The soldiers' families lived outside the fort. Some of the soldiers probably lived there, too.

As well as keeping guard on the Antonine Wall, the soldiers were also able to relax. At the bath house they met their friends and played games like dice.

Source 1 ▶
This stone was found at Old Kilpatrick fort on the Antonine Wall. Can you see the words IVLIO CANDIDO? Julius Candidus was a centurion of the First Legion Italica.

▼ **Source 2**
At Bar Hill fort on the Antonine Wall, archaeologists found bits of many things used by the Romans. These pictures show you what they looked like. Some of them were found in the well at the fort.

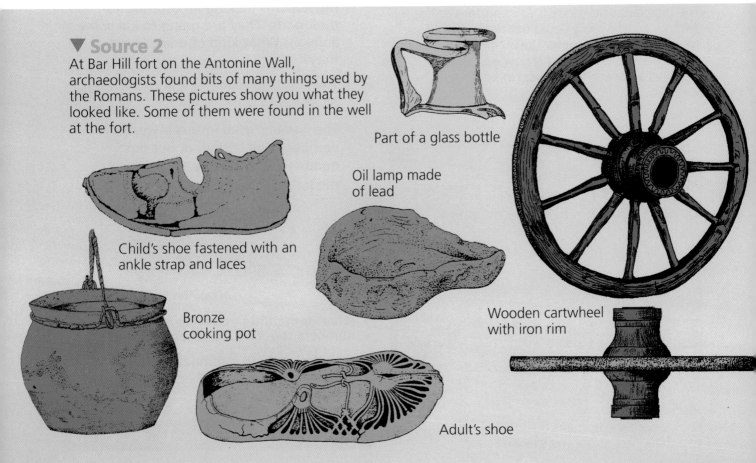

Part of a glass bottle

Oil lamp made of lead

Child's shoe fastened with an ankle strap and laces

Bronze cooking pot

Wooden cartwheel with iron rim

Adult's shoe

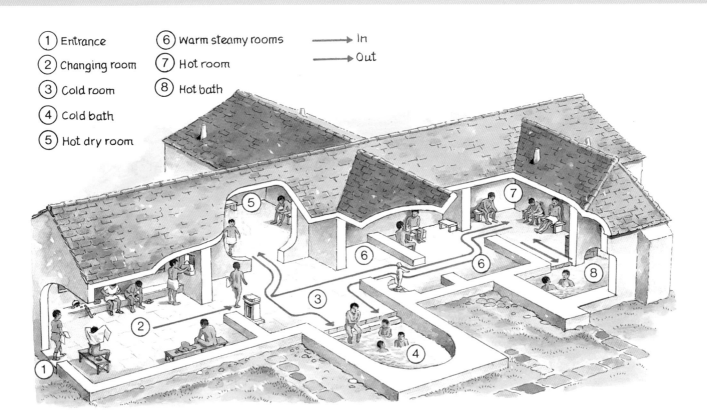

① Entrance
② Changing room
③ Cold room
④ Cold bath
⑤ Hot dry room
⑥ Warm steamy rooms
⑦ Hot room
⑧ Hot bath

⟶ In
⟶ Out

▲ Source 3

This is a plan of the Roman bath house found at Bearsden fort. Follow the arrows to find your way round. A Roman bath house had different kinds of bath inside it. There were hot and cold rooms and hot and cold baths, a bit like a modern sauna. People went to the baths to meet their friends as well as get clean. Sometimes they would play games like dice when they were in the warm rooms. People can still visit the bath house at Bearsden today. This chapter will help you imagine what it was like when the Romans lived there.

1 **Imagine you are an archaeologist. Look carefully at page 28. Using the evidence find three things you can say about life at a fort.**

2 **Design a leaflet which shows how the bath house would have been used.**

A C T I V I T I E S

store house or stable
gate
barracks
grain stores
barracks
workshop
store
bath house
toilets
gate

▲ Source 4
This shows you what Bearsden Fort on the Antonine Wall looked like.

In 1978, archaeologists finished excavating Leckie Broch near Stirling. The broch was a large stone tower. It stood between two rivers. It would have looked a very important place to natives and Romans alike. This was once the home of a **rich** and **important** family.

The people of the Broch, and the families who lived nearby, grew crops and kept **sheep** and cattle. In the winter, the women would spin the sheep fleeces and **weave** them into woollen cloth to keep everyone warm.

There was probably a village **smith** who used **iron** to make **tools** for farming, and **weapons** for the soldiers. Iron was stronger than bronze. Both the Romans and the local people used iron by now.

The families could **trade** their crops with the Romans at the nearby fort. In exchange they could get luxury goods like beautiful Roman jewellery, glass jugs and cups, or fine pottery. They could also get useful everyday things like lamps, spindles to spin the fleece, and loom weights for weaving.

Life at Leckie Broch came to sudden end in a fire. Archaeologists cannot agree what caused it. Some think that it might have been a Roman attack, while others think that it might have been an accident.

◀ **Source 1**
This picture of the Broch of Mousa in Shetland shows you what a broch looked like. It would have had a thatched roof.

1 **Look at the words in black boxes. Now look at all the pictures on these two pages. Can you say which pictures give us the evidence for each of the black box words?**

   For example: How do we know they were rich**? They could afford luxury things like glass bracelets.**

2 **Using all the evidence on these pages, imagine you were living at Leckie Broch. Decide whether you are one of the rich owners, a farm servant, a smith or a soldier. Write what you think a day in your life might have been like. Draw a picture to go with your story.**

ACTIVITIES

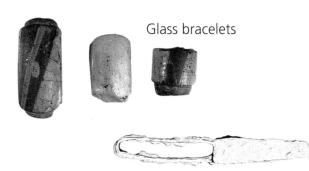

Glass bracelets

Iron scissors (called sheep shears)
for cutting wool off sheep

Loom weights (look back at page 11)

Iron spear and sword

Iron foot plough

▲ Source 2
All these things were found at Leckie Broch. They
were all made by local people.

Roman pottery

Roman mirror
made of shiny
silvery bronze

▲ Source 3
Some of the things found at Leckie Broch came
from the Romans. Some are everyday household
things. Other things (like the mirror), are luxury
things which the people did not really need for
their everyday life.

The mirror looked like this

The Picts

About 1500 years ago, Scotland was inhabited by the Britons, the Scots, the Picts and the Angles. Each group wanted to be the most powerful and there were many battles. The most important was the Battle of Nechtansmere in 685 AD. From about the fifth century until about the ninth, the Picts were the most important people and ruled the largest part of Scotland.

▼ **Source 1**
Scotland around 600 AD.

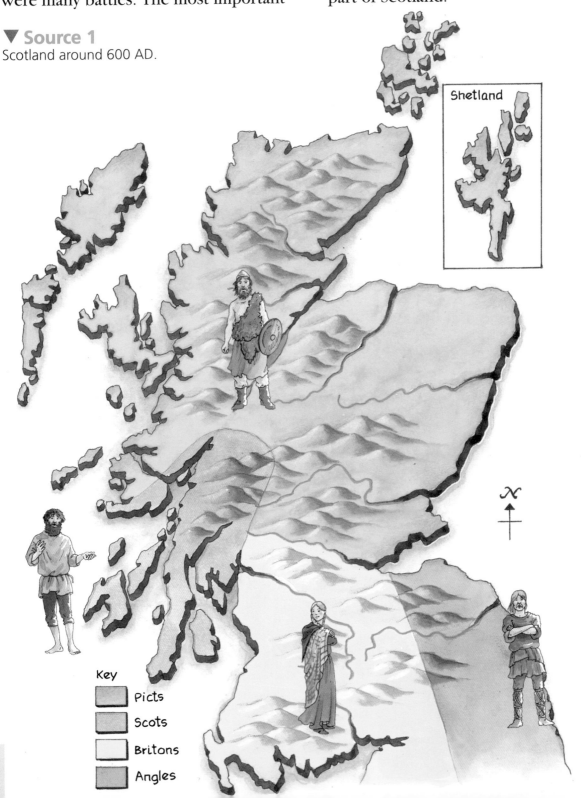

Shetland

Key

- ▢ Picts
- ▢ Scots
- ▢ Britons
- ▢ Angles

▼ Source 2

After the Battle of Nechtansmere in 685 AD:

1 Slowly we make our way home from battle. We are weary but we are also proud. We have defeated the Angles at Nechtansmere. Now we Picts are more powerful.

2 Back in our village we celebrate with a great feast. The village craftsmen listen to our battle tales. They will carve pictures in stone to tell our story.

3 The everyday work of the village goes on. We need more fields for our animals and crops. We need wood for houses, boats and things like bowls and tool handles.

4 The women make warm clothes and bedding from animal hide. The fishermen use hide too. They make waterproof skins for their boats.

5 We must keep a watch at all times. The Scots of Dalriada want our lands. But tonight all is still, and we can rest.

1 **Look at the settlements shown in Source 1. Why were these good places to settle?**

2 **Look at a modern map of Scotland. What makes a good place to live now?**

3 **Find where you live on Source 1. Which tribe would you have belonged to?**

A C T I V I T I E S

A Story in Stone

The Picts were very important for over 500 years. They were very artistic. They covered special stones in wonderful carvings. They might then have painted the carvings in bright colours. Some of these Pictish stones still stand in many parts of Scotland. One of the finest stands at Aberlemno, near Forfar. It was made in the eighth century, and it tells the story of the battle you have just read about on pages 32 and 33 – the Battle of Nechtansmere in 685 AD, between the Picts and the Angles.

Source 1 ▶

This is the Aberlemno stone. Pictish craftsmen used a hammer, punch and chisel to carve the stone, and then a stone tool to make it smooth. Look carefully at the top of the stone. Can you see the heads of two snarling beasts?

Notice the shape of the letter Z on its side and the large circle with two smaller circles. The Picts often carved these shapes. They are called symbols. One is known as the Z-rod. The other is called the triple disc. No-one knows what they mean. The pictures on the stone are laid out like a cartoon strip. They tell the story of the battle.

Source 2 ▶

This helmet once belonged to one of the Picts' enemies, called an Angle. It was found in England in 1982. It dates from the eighth century. Can you see helmets like this on the stone?

◀ Source 3

One warrior is chasing another. Which do you think is the Pict? Why? The warrior being chased has thrown his sword and shield away. Can you find them?

◀ Source 4

A group of warriors on foot attacks a man on horseback. The first warrior holds his shield to protect himself, and his sword ready to slash at his enemy. The second warrior in the group holds a spear ready to protect the first man. His shield hangs from his shoulder on leather straps. The third man stands ready to take over from the second.

◀ Source 5

Two enemies fight on horseback with spears and swords. The last picture on the right shows what happened to one of them. Why do you think the large raven is shown?

1 **Look closely at sources 3, 4 and 5. Write the story of the battle in your own words.**

2 **Draw and label the different types of weapons you can see on the stone.**

A C T I V I T I E S

A Pictish Stone Today

Near the town of Forres in Moray stands the magnificent Sueno's Stone. It is 6.5 metres high and is the tallest stone in Scotland. The stone was discovered nearly four hundred years ago and at that time was given the name Sueno's Stone. No-one really knows why the stone was put up or when it was carved. The beautiful curling patterns are very specially Pictish. You can see them on other stones, and on Pictish silver and jewellery that has been found.

Like many other Pictish stones, Sueno's Stone has been worn away over hundreds of years by the weather and by pollution. Stones must be protected if they are to survive. They may be put in a museum or, like Sueno's Stone, they can be protected where they stand. Sueno's Stone has been covered by a glass shell. Although this protects the stone, many people dislike it.

Source 1 ▶
Sueno's Stone. Since this picture was taken, the stone has been covered by a glass shell.

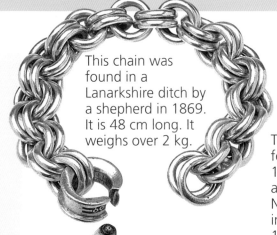

This chain was found in a Lanarkshire ditch by a shepherd in 1869. It is 48 cm long. It weighs over 2 kg.

This pin was found over 100 years ago at Norrie's Law in Fife. it is 17 cm long.

These are *almost* identical. They come from Norrie's Law in Fife. Each one is 9 cm long, and 4 cm wide. They weigh about 80g each.

ACTIVITIES

1 Use the chapter on Pictish stones (page 34) to help you read Sueno's Stone on page 36. What might the figures at the foot of the cross be doing?

2 In Source 1 on this page you can see some of the pictures on the back of Sueno's stone. What do they show?

3 Now that you have looked closely at Sueno's Stone, use what you have learned to write an information board for visitors. Don't forget illustrations!

4 Weather and pollution are damaging many Pictish stones. Do you think this matters? Give a reason for your answer.

5 Some people dislike the glass shell which protects Sueno's Stone. Why do you think this is? Can you think of a better way to protect it? Design and make a model of your idea.

▲ Source 2

All these precious silver things are Pictish. Can you say why? Look at their sizes and shapes. What do you think they were used for?

▼ Source 1

The back of Sueno's Stone.

19

Scots from Ireland

You are a Scot in the ninth century AD. Your grandfather tells you the story of your people:

1 Our ancestors sailed from Ireland and landed on the western shores here. They named their new home Dalriada. They hunted the wild animals with dogs and longbows.

2 They built fine forts as defence against the enemy, and named them in our own Gaelic tongue. They fought many battles against the Picts, the Angles and the Vikings from Norway. Some people began to move east to escape the Viking raids.

3 In 839 AD, Vikings killed the King of the Picts and the Pictish throne came to the Scots. Many Scots moved east into Pictland.

4 Gaelic became the main language of Highland Scotland. In 843 AD our ruler Kenneth mac Alpin became the first King of Scotland.

That is the end of one story but also the beginning of a new one. You should be proud to be a Scot!

5

1 Look back at the map on page 32. In which part of Scotland did the Scots settle north, south, east or west?

2 What forced the Scots to extend their lands at first?

A C T I V I T I E S

Life in a Scottish Fort

Source 1 ▶
Dunadd Fort today. Dunadd was an important Scottish fort from the seventh to the ninth century.

I am a watchman at Dunadd Fort – welcome! This is one of the finest forts we have built since we came to Dalriada from Ireland.

It is high up on a hill so that I have a good view across the flat, boggy land. I can also see the River Add, which leads to the sea.

There is great excitement today. The King will arrive soon! Dunadd is very special to him, for this is where he stepped into the carved footprint and became Ruler of the Scots.

Inside the fort, everyone is busy. The store master has chosen barrels of the best beer. He has brought out sides of venison which have been smoked over the winter. In the great hall the logs are piled high on the fire and the long tables are set for a feast.

But, look – I must go, here comes the King!"

1 Imagine you are a Scot building a fort. Plan where you will build it. List the reasons why it is a good place.

2 **Dun** was the Scots word for a small fort. Find Dunadd on a map of Scotland. List any other place names beginning with Dun that you can find.

3 In a group, act out the scenes described on these pages.

4 Describe how you prepare for a special occasion in your house.

A C T I V I T I E S

▲ **Source 3**
The King stepped into the footprint of kings before him.

Changing Faiths

All the people in this book so far were non-Christians. They worshipped animals, the stars and the sun. So why did people change to a Christian way of life?

People who travel and teach about God to non-Christians are called **missionaries**. The first Christian missionary to Scotland was called Ninian. In the fifth century, he built a church at Whithorn on the Solway coast. The church was called Candida Casa, or the white house. From here, missionaries travelled round the country spreading the Christian message. People were attracted to this new religion. It was based on peace and love. It promised eternal life for everyone, rich or poor.

▲ Source 1

In AD 563, another important Christian missionary arrived in Scotland. Columba sailed across the sea from Ireland. He settled on the island of Iona and built a church.

Source 2 ▶

This stone at Meigle in Perthshire shows the Bible story of Daniel in the lions' den.

▲ Source 3
This stone at Glamis in Angus is probably the oldest one to show a cross. Can you also see some Pictish things?

▼ Source 4
This cross is at Eassie. Can you see the angels carved on the stone?

The change to Christianity took hundreds of years. Slowly, carvings on stones changed from only Pictish patterns and pictures. The pictures became a mixture of Pictish and Christian ones. Finally, only Christian symbols appear. By about 750 AD, most people living in Scotland were Christian.

1 Prepare a talk on how and why the Scots became Christians.

2 Use clay to make your own carved 'stone'. Either show both Christian and Pictish pictures or show a Bible story.

3 Think about the place where you live. What evidence is there to show that Christianity is the most common religion in Scotland today?

ACTIVITIES

The Holy Island of Iona

In the last chapter you learned that Christian missionaries settled on the island of Iona. They were all men who wanted to spend their lives working for God. Men who do this are called **monks**. They built a church and big rooms where they could all eat and sleep. This kind of church is called a **monastery**.

The monks lived a simple but hardworking life. Much of their time was spent teaching about Christianity, or in quiet prayer. They wore tunics of rough cloth, and leather sandals.

The monks shared the daily tasks. They grew vegetables and herbs in the garden. In the fields animals grazed and crops grew. Some monks were skilled carpenters and carved beautiful wooden crosses.

▼ Source 1

Iona may have looked like this in Columba's time. Here, the artist has shown the monastery being attacked by invaders. Turn to page 44 to find out who they were.

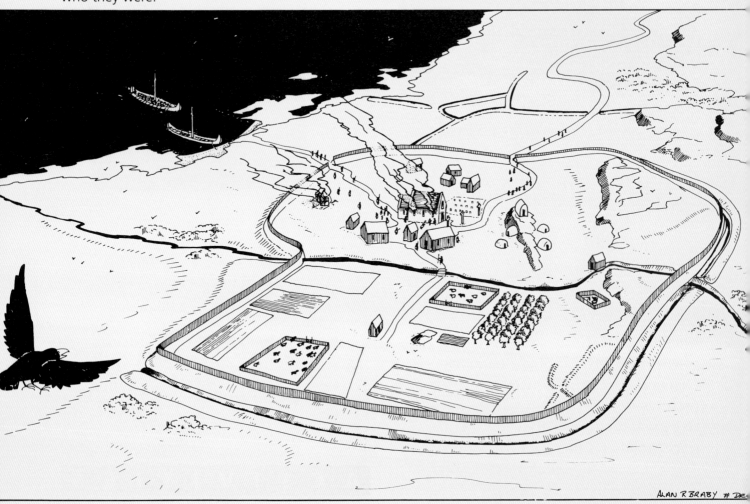

ALAN R BRABY # DE

▲ Source 2
Iona Abbey as it is today.

One of the first things the monks had to do when they arrived on Iona was to build. To keep out the strong winds, walls were made of woven twigs covered with mud and straw, called **wattle**. The most important building was the church. But there was also a house for visitors to the island, a dining hall, and a kitchen where the monks prepared meals. The monks slept in small stone rooms called **cells**.

Iona was an important Christian centre not only because of the monastery, but also because from here the monks carried Christianity to other parts of Scotland. Today, Iona is still an important place for Christians.

1 **Why do you think Columba chose to settle on an island?**

2 **If you were a monk, what would be the good things about living on an island? What sort of problems might there be?**

3 **Do you have daily tasks at home or at school? Are any the same as the monks' tasks?**

A C T I V I T I E S

Invaders from the North

Many places in Scotland still have their Norse names. Here are some of them:

-wick = bay

-ay = island

-dale = valley

-bister or -bster = farm

-ness or -nish = headland

-ding or -ting = parliament place

There are some names on the map on page 45. Can you think of more?

Towards the end of the eighth century, new and terrible invaders arrived in Scotland – the Vikings from Norway.

From the icy lands in the North, the Vikings set sail in their magnificent longships. They came in many boatloads to surprise the enemy, then raid the farms and monasteries. Nothing stopped them in their search for treasure, cattle and slaves. In AD 795, the fearless Norsemen landed on the holy island of Iona. Terrified, the monks ran for their lives as the raiders grabbed the gold and silver cups and plates from the monastery. The Vikings drove animals from the farms onto their longships, killing anyone who tried to stop them. This was only one of many dreadful attacks on the north and west of Scotland.

At first, the Vikings came only to raid, but they found that the land in this new country was much more fertile than the high mountains and deep forests of their homeland. Many decided to settle here. They brought their wives and families and built homes. Some of these can still be seen today, such as Jarlshof in Shetland. The Vikings were here to stay!

◀ **Source 1**
A Viking raider.

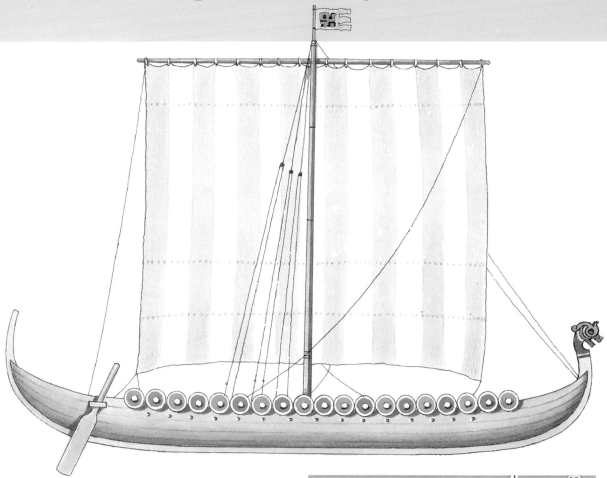

▲ Source 2

This drawing shows you what a Viking warship looked like. Boatloads of Vikings attacked the north and west coast of Scotland.

1 **Look at source 3, and a modern map of Scotland. Name four of the main areas of Viking settlement.**

2 **Use the information in this chapter to write about why the first Viking attacks took place, and why the Vikings decided to settle in Scotland.**

3 **Make up a cartoon showing a Viking raid, from the journey in the longboat to leaving with the treasure.**

4 **Make a timeline showing the settlers of Scotland up to the time of the Vikings. Illustrate each section.**

A C T I V I T I E S

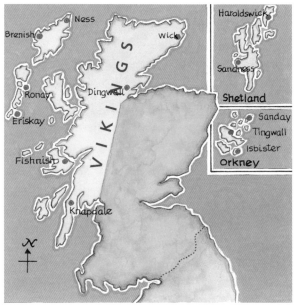

▲ Source 3

This map shows where the Vikings settled in Scotland. Norse was the language of the Northern Isles until the late sixteenth century. Many places still have their Norse names, such as Tingwall in Orkney. The Viking Parliament was called the Ting, and Tingwall was where it met.

Viking Settlers

Viking settlers lived in long houses like the one shown here. Little houses were added outside for animals and for storing food. A house like this was called an *ut-hus* by the Vikings. Does this remind you of a word we use today?

The settlers kept cows, pigs, sheep and hens. They hunted fish and seabirds. They salted their meat and smoked their fish to keep it longer. As well as meat, the animals provided wool and leather for clothing. Their bones made combs and pins. The settlers grew barley, oats and flax in the fields. The fibres from the flax were used to make linen for the long Viking robes.

▲ **Source 1**
A Viking long house may have looked like this.

> Our people sailed to Scotland from Norway. There is good farming land here for our animals and crops, and so we have made this our home. We work hard all day, and in the evening we play board games and tell stories of brave Viking warriors.

> I help with feeding the animals and hoeing the crops. I learn about the history of my people by listening to poems and stories.

Source 2 ▶
Vikings told their history by using story poems called sagas. A famous one is called the Orkneyinga Saga.

Discovering the Past

In this book, you have learned about the many different people who settled in Scotland. We know about these early settlers because of evidence which has been left behind, such as carved stones or the remains of buildings.

As you have discovered, exploring the past can help us find out more about our history and also about the way we live now. You don't have to be a historian or an archaeologist to find out about the past. Here are some activities for you to try.

Be a detective! Visit a historic site near where you live. How much can you learn just by looking?

Make up an illustrated guidebook showing interesting evidence to look at, such as a carved symbol.

Look around your village or town. You will be surprised how many clues to the past you will find. Don't forget to look in the graveyard!

Finally, look at a modern building. What will detectives of the future be able to tell about our lifestyle?

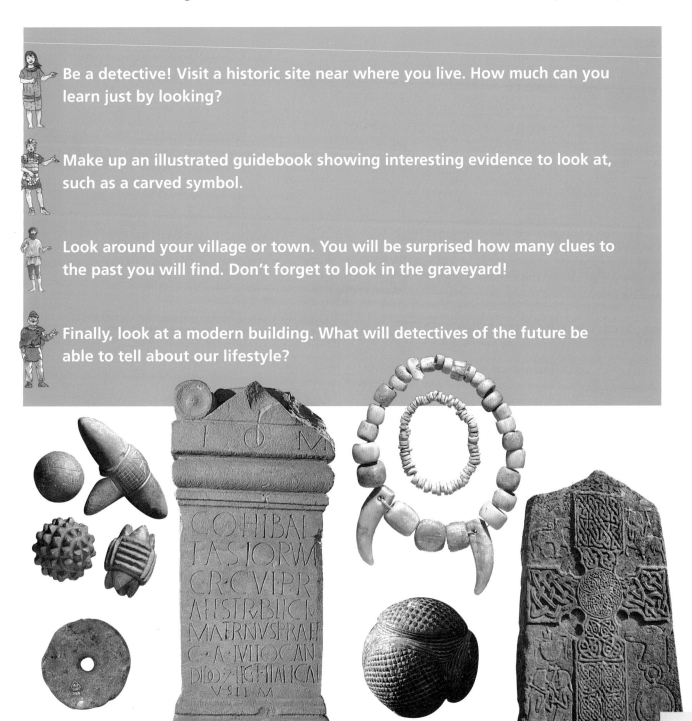

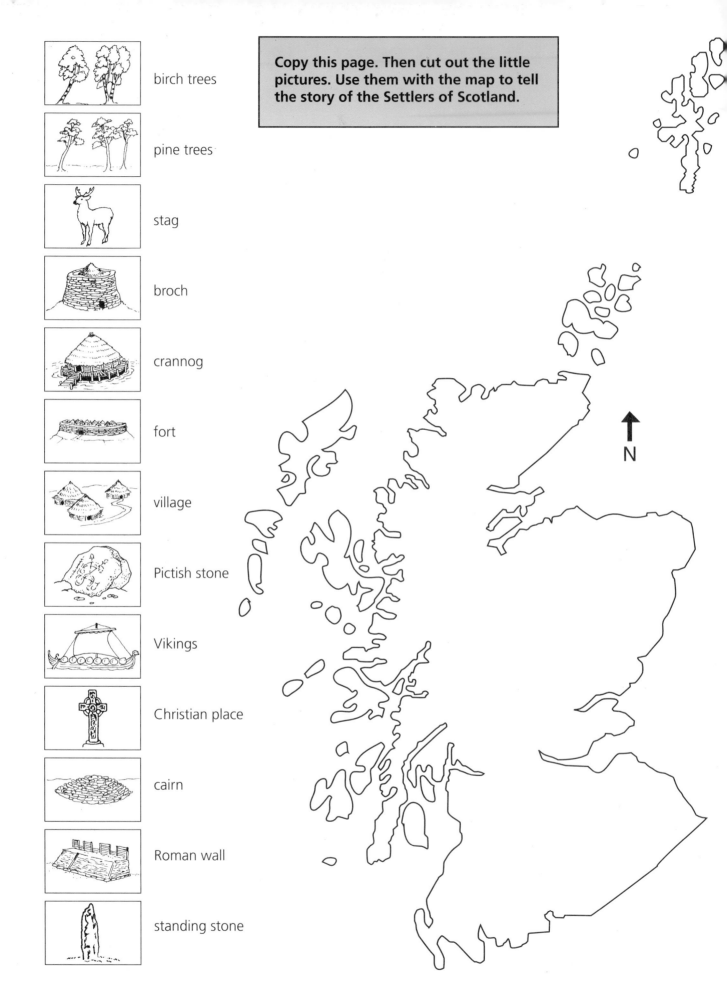

birch trees

pine trees

stag

broch

crannog

fort

village

Pictish stone

Vikings

Christian place

cairn

Roman wall

standing stone

Copy this page. Then cut out the little pictures. Use them with the map to tell the story of the Settlers of Scotland.

N